POTRY

Potry

A Collection of Stoned Poems

JENET . LE LACHEUR

Reconnecting Rainbows Press

Published in the United Kingdom
by Reconnecting Rainbows Press

First published in paperback in 2024

Copyright © Jenet E. Le Lacheur, 2024

The right of Jenet Le Lacheur to be identified as the author of this book has been asserted by her in accordance with the Copyright, Designs and Patents Act 1988.

All rights reserved. No part of this publication may be reproduced, stored in a retrieval system, or transmitted, in any form, or by any means (electronic, mechanical, photocopying, recording or otherwise) without the prior written permission of the publisher, nor be otherwise circulated in any form of binding or cover other than that in which it is published and without a similar condition being imposed on the subsequent purchaser.

Printed and bound by Ingram Spark

"These unguarded moments are truly beautiful and funny and horny and all of the things that I absolutely adore. This collection feels like an invitation to a sleepover... with all the giggles, secrets, warmth and fun that implies.'

- Girl on the Net

Contents

FOREWORD

BRING ON THE ROCKS, OR DON'T

INTRODUCTION

I

II

Foreword

MAZ HEDGEHOG

I was created in a lab specifically to piss off *Daily Mail* readers; I'm a fat Black autistic polyam kinky bisexual agender femme lesbian.

I am also a poet with two collections out (*Vivat Regina, The Body in Its Seasons*) and one anthology (Tell Me Who We Were Before Life Made Us). I am a 'theatre maker', which is a rather pretentious way of saying that I wear several different hats – actor, playwright, director, producer – because I can't get any one of them to pay enough to live on. In truth though, I am just some bitch. I am some bitch who really loves poetry and has been tasked with writing a foreword.

How to describe this collection? How to place it in its proper context? It's bananas, dancing on the edge where 'surreal' becomes 'utterly fucking ridiculous' and I love it for that. Jenet revels in kink (cloaca themed erotica, anyone) and politics (because SWERFs can truly get fucked) and the careful, careless vulnerability of relationships. Some may call this collection 'raw', but that would be too simple. It is curated, bringing together a dozen strands of Jenet's artistic sensibilities into a slim volume that demands everything of its readers, or nothing. You'll get out what you put in, and I mean that in the filthiest way possible.

The collection feels a little like a cubist epic poem, meant to convey myriad facets of Jenet's mind at once. When she says it was written over the course of a year, I believe it. If she said they'd all been written in a weekend, I'd believe it. Not because they feel rushed or underwritten, but because they feel so very present, so very of one mind. The journey in it isn't really one through time, but through the many rooms of a single house.

The poems are all short, almost ascetic in their brevity. I'm normally a fan of the kind of vast sprawling poems favoured by the stuffiest of early twentieth century literature professors (think Paradise Lost, The Iliad and The Lady of Shalott), and spend a lot of time wishing poems were longer. But not here; Jenet uses a couple lines at a time as a vehicle for a delightfully lush hedonism. The collection is bare, but not remotely cold. Somehow – and don't ask me how – she finds room for warmth, humour, rage, bitterness and a bunch of other feelings besides. I've laughed and I've winced. I've felt both seen and beautifully alienated.

All in all, the collection feels almost like a DIY dungeon, cobbled together from half a dozen trips to B&Q and Pets at Home. Its sparse, even spartan, form is there to take you to gorgeously extreme places. Don't take it too seriously, or do. Neither I nor Jenet are going to tell you what to do.

Bring on the Rocks, or Don't

JOHN HENRY FALLE

How do I know Jenet? Well she and I share geology.

Don't get me wrong, we were made on different islands (hers Guernsey and mine Jersey) but what we share is a river of mud that has run its slow course from Antarctica to what's now the English Channel over the last half a billion years and change, running at roughly the speed of your fingernails. Our mud and blood siblings are the East Midlands and the Iberian Peninsula, our home the shale humps that loomed over the only recently drowned grass plains of mammoth hunting grounds (what the archaeologists are already calling La Manche Land). We shared the river run bowl of London for many years (have you ever looked out from the twenty-sixth floor at University College Hospital on a clear day? You can see it from up there) before she escaped, hopping the rim via the Elizabeth Line Line to look for new strata and plot her own geologic events.

I have only seen a few of Jenet's faces (as an actor, she collects them); perhaps you can see some of them in this book. There are faultlines I know that are shot through this book I hope you're holding. How to investigate a landscape by dancing across its surface. How to tell jokes to bounce like LiDAR waves across it, no pun unpunned. How to love wildly to get to something true beneath the top layer of earth or look for blobs of missing or watch for gulls in your peripheral vision or just observe an abyss in such a way that it might actually fill us up.

'Let's go'.

Introduction

Up until the age of thirty I was completely straightedge.

And I'd been abstaining in other areas too.

Barring one or two paid commissions, in the four years prior to hitting the big three-o I'd written all of one (1) poem. Don't ask me why something I'd used to do so prodigiously had fallen so far from my authorial ambit. Maybe in my characteristically wanky way I felt I'd exhausted all the interesting things to do with the medium. I'm a whore for constraints – and a whore for *re*straints too, but we'll come to that – and over the decade I was churning out poetry on the reg I voraciously partook of every seemingly insurmountable impediment to writing them I could lay my hands on. These included, but were not limited to:

Improvised sonnets, monosyllabic sonnets, monovocalic sonnets which used only a single vowel ('*Egrets feed whenever they feel the need / They sweep the slender neck 'tween reedy ferns / They feel between the deep, fermented weeds*') and conversely, lipographic sonnets, which entirely avoided said vowel.

Fair to say I had a thing for sonnets.

Next, the paradelle, a form allegedly invented in eleventh century France, but in fact conceived – apocryphal backstory and all – by US poet Billy Collins in the late nineties to parody needlessly complicated fixed forms and intended to be impossible. And lo and behold I wrote one that *made fucking sense*, plus a couple of villanelles for good measure.

Take it from me, do not go gentle into that poetic form.

I wrote palindromic haikus, just for shits and gigs ('*Hannah won desserts / Hey, but no spoon (oops) on tub! / Yeh, stressed now, Hannah*'), tongue twisters, head scratchers, a poem where every line was made up of a prime number of characters and, last but not least, a sprawling, days-long project (another sonnet, our old fave), each line of which was an anagram of the morbidly appropriate title, *Every Cloud Hath a Silver Lining.*

'A heaving liver loudly retches in

Convulsing evilly her hated air

Lo, vile lurches have a trying din

Unvalvéd ire clog the shiny lair'

I stopped after that.

You must bear in mind of course that every one of these bastard children came into the world for pleasure rather than profit (I'm something of a masochist, so my idea of pleasure is pretty skewed at the best of times), and I never intended them for performance or publication.

At its heart this whole endeavour was just an outlet for my overactive brain. So given the nature of escalation once I was in the poetic equivalent of bloodsports stepped in so far that returning were as tedious as go o'er, the thought of reverting to poems without some convoluted gimmick to lend a frisson of impossibility left me cold.

But I digress.

Up until the age of thirty I was completely straightedge.

The odd traumatic experience with alcohol in my youth had always meant that I sought my kicks from other more baroque sources. These included, and really were limited to, art, word games, snapping an especially aesthetic shot of a vivip lizard or grass snake while out herping, and being beaten and degraded to what felt like an inch of my life in a remote dungeon in Bilsthorpe. With the commencement of hormone therapy however a seismic shift occurred, both physically and mentally. As if by magic something that had always been prohibitively anxiety-inducing – putting drug-adjacent substances in my meatsack – was demystified overnight.

It was around this time I sucked my first dick, and immediately found it to be not only my drug of choice (when attached to a cute girl, at least) but also something from which I could make a decent living. HRT: the real gateway substance.

Yet another sea change occurred when I first used botanical aids to indulge my bimbofication kink – enforced airheadedness? Sign me the eff up – and found myself compelled to take up my metaphorical pen and start fucking with poems again.

At first I just wanted to capture the vivid hallucinations of a priorly sober woman having her mind nudged into different spheres of consciousness for the first time in three decades (I wasn't even on psychedelics, but during my first outing my metamour's foot became a sasquatch and I laughed for a full five minutes about how hilarious this would be if I found it funny instead of terrifying). Soon though, every absurd or quasi-profound thing that popped into my head was deemed worthy of putting down on the page. Hence this bitch, *Potry*.

The pieces in this volume span a year of my life, from January 2022-23. I've split it into two parts for no other reason than it felt right and it pleased me, which, in addition to the unwavering faith and steadfast cheerleading of my publisher Ash Brockwell, is also the reason this book exists at all.

For better, or for worse.

A final word. Be aware as you peruse the pages of this poetical pantheon that herein lies my mind *at its most unguarded*. Much of it even I don't understand. But as I said to the more vocal opponents of my first fringe play, an absurdist romp about a pseudo-Beckettian boob who wakes up one day to be greeted by a world composed entirely of frog: try not to think about it.

Instead, do what I so often struggle with, and feel. Like a star-nosed mole in its burrow, build up a three-dimensional model of a strange woman's emotional landscape using the twenty-two fleshy appendages that surround your muzzle.

You know, like poetry's all about.

I

One

Purple mist all around
Illuminated by a haze of bright pink fireflies
Beneath the scanty shade of a gently bending willow tree
The scene plays out; the scene is you and me

Moorhen

Is a male moorhen a moorhen?
Or is it a moorcock?
I would like it, as a name
I would love moorcock
Perhaps we could get it added
To the dictionary?
Can we have moorcock?
Please?

Your Face

Your face is on about its
Fifth
Face of the evening

The Story of Balamory

I wrote the story of balamory
I wrote the story of balamory in my own blood
On the runes of a crumbling civilisation
I scrawled the story of balamory atop the razed
Ruins of a once great people
Screaming all the while for death to free me
From the tyranny
Of knowing
The story of balamory

The God-Renny

You come to me on Trans Day of Visibility
And you ask me to kill terves for money
And you do not even think to use my proper pronouns

I'm gonna give them some hormones they can't refuse

Is lead a hormone?

Please Hold

Please hold onto the handrail
Please do not dislodge the handrail from your hand
An excision of said handrail from your hand
Ought not to be on the cards
Keep those digits railed
Think you can handle this rail?
Think again
Hold

When You Do It

When you do it
Do it with a smile
I want to see your glee
At sanctioning my demise
Hold that blade beneath my chin
And whisper 'yield to me'
And I'll smile back
As I say 'no'
Brat

And you reduce/complete me

High Coo for Polys

You're my entire world
And I have five entire worlds
How lucky am I

Metamours

I've five metamours I've never met
Which seems strange
Makes one fret
A metamour, I get
A metamour is an amour
Whom I'm meant to have met

Right?

Ephemeral

I am ephemeral
And my inner thigh
Is a femoral
And the message of this poem
Is a femme moral:

Life's short. Get in my thighs

Femme Oral?

Do you wanna?

Crunchy Slut Porn Flakes

Crack your knuckles
Show me how bad it's going to be for me
Wrap yourself around me
Then destroy me

Bit

By

Bit

Tautonym Court Road

Elizabeth Line?
Or Elizabeth Line Line?
No-one seems to know

A Lighter Note

The plants outside the living room window
Are growing
If left unchecked
They'll engulf the whole place
Till no-one can get in or out
And maybe then
The world will stop
For me at least

I hope

Have You Fucking Tasted Strawberries Though?

Have you fucking tasted strawberries though
Have you fucking tasted strawberries though
This poem is called
'Have You Fucking Tasted Strawberries Though?'
Because have you fucking tasted strawberries though

The Dragon of Me

Enter the dragon of me
Insert yourself into my cloaca
Fertilise my leathery eggs
I'll keep them all
At just the right temperature
For them to be what they want to be
And if we find ourselves
With a female army
We'll parthenogenetically rise

II

Two

Curple twists, falls to ground
Eviscerated in a blaze of high-pitched lupine cries
As teeth and fangs pervade the silence,
rending the fallow deer
The scene fades out, and there's no more to fear

Swerf and Miss Me with That Shit

Sure
I dress like a streetwalker

Every time I wear clothes
I'm necessarily
Dressing like a streetwalker

That's the beauty of it

Shite Wilderness

Do you hear the lemmings
Bidding us to not follow them over the cliff?
Their paws were forced in the name of entertainment
We have no such fetters
If we but free ourselves

Poor lemmings

I'm Just a Tranny in a Diaper

What do I know?
I'm just a tranny in a diaper
Pontification is for pontiffs
And people who say 'pontification'

I wrote a poetry anthology
And I still don't think
You should listen to me
What does that say?

Nothing hopefully

To My Vagina

I don't have you yet
And it sucks
I want to put you in me
And then put you to work
You magnificent fuck

But instead I'm talking to a man
Who doesn't even
KNOW
How to induce lactation
Fuck my life

*

You make me feel safe
You make me feel seen
You make me feel sated

I think we could give each other a quiet life

Don't you?

Gaps!

Gaps!
That's what they're called!
Gaps!
Not blobs of missing

Eye's Bird View

My eyelashes are so heavy
They make gulls in the periphery of my vision
Larus ocularis
Flapping and diving
In the water of my tears

Enjoymbment

Let me be your servant
Your cook and your coquette
Rest your weary head
And I'll
Help you get

To
The end
Of your day

Hike Who?

Cis men's actions must
Be accounted for, woman!
Explain themselves! >:(

Getting Up

Definitely getting up
The Getting Up project has been greenlit
The money's in place
The investors are stoked
We have an amazing roster of talent attached

Get the fuck up, essentially

Gotten Up

Rave reviews
Roger Ebert dot com calls it
'An ascension from bed to carpet
That's literally all you can say about it'
Stars

Getting Up in the Morning

A sprawling project
It'll development hell
For some years to come

Out of Hand: A Getting Up Story

The tetralogy was out of control
Plagued by diminishing returns
And creative bankruptcy

But most egregiously

People kept calling it a 'quadrilogy'

Saturday Night

Three trans girls
One neopussy

Each doing edibles
One with a joint

In other words
(As one observed)

Two blunts
And two points

Like an Ending

I'm leaping off a cliff
In the dark
I'll either be dashed on igneous shards
Of my island home

Or meet the cool sea
Slice through
Painless
Effortless, at home

Like a gannet's bone
Helmet
And become a mermaid, flourishing
In my submarine home

Set for life

Bring on the rocks, or don't

Let's go

www.ingramcontent.com/pod-product-compliance
Lightning Source LLC
Chambersburg PA
CBHW050209130526
44590CB00043B/3358